Self-Esteem

A Practical Manual For Conquering Self-doubt And Insecurity, Cultivating Enhanced Confidence And Inner Resilience And Uncover Your Latent Abilities And Transform Your Life Within A 30-Day Period

Walker Pena

TABLE OF CONTENT

The Reality Of Low Self-Worth 1

Self-Respectdo You Really Want To Know? 7

Setting Goals Is Essential 14

Tips For Developing Self-Esteem That Values You Both Internally And Outer 39

Establishing Healthy Border 44

Essential Human Fears 58

Science Of Goodwill 70

Compassion For Self-Reflection 82

How Much Do I Believe In Myself? 100

What Self-Esteem Means 115

Discovering Your Personal Story 132

Definition Of Self-Esteem 158

The Reality Of Low Self-Worth

The reality regarding the term "self-esteem" is sometimes overused in the context of personal growth. For many years, self-help books have focused on raising one's self-esteem, and a lot of people still associate success, happiness, and well-being with having high self-esteem. As things stand, though, psychologists are questioning the purported benefits of raising self-esteem more and more.

To put it simply, self-esteem is the degree to which we approve of ourselves. It's a word that encompasses our whole subjective sense of value and worth. People who have high self-esteem usually think well of themselves and are much more accepting of who they are.

Nonetheless, it should come as no surprise that many people have viewed having a strong sense of self-worth as a sign of wellness. When we think positively about ourselves, we might feel, think, and act happier and healthier than when we think badly about ourselves.

The benefits of having a high sense of self-worth have been extensively discussed in scholarly research and even in the media. Numerous educational institutions have implemented programs designed to foster self-worth. Perhaps the most well-known is a large-scale program in California called the

California Task Force to Promote Self-Esteem. However, boosting self-esteem is really difficult. Most of us have this incredibly strong, enduring trait that is difficult to change because our perceptions of ourselves are so ingrained.

We have an extremely difficult time letting go of our preconceived notions and definitions of who we are. Whether that's good or bad. The well-known self-compassion researcher Kristin Neff suggests that working to raise one's self-esteem could have negative consequences. Boosting self-esteem with gratuitous praise or affirmations may obscure chances for personal development and unhealthy or ineffective behaviours that must be changed on their own.

Sustaining a high sense of self-worth has also been linked to racism, bullying, narcissism, and superiority complexes, as well as an inflated sense of self. Comparing and evaluating ourselves against others can also lead to us putting people down to feel better about ourselves or even elevating them to make ourselves feel worse.

It stands to reason that the most vulnerable would be those with low self-esteem. Strangely, Neff shows how those who have a high sense of self-worth are also at risk. She gives the example of a student receiving a B rather than an A grade to illustrate how any failure can seem like a huge blow. Self-esteem can shift significantly, especially if it is dependent on one's success in specific spheres of life, such as one's career, relationships, parenting style, etc. When we perform well in some areas, our self-esteem rises, but when we don't, it falls, which makes it unstable and likely to be harmful to our well-being.

Many of us are riding this rollercoaster. But what happens if we wish to exit? We all probably have some level of self-esteem, and it's definitely not zero. But if it's essentially fixed and we still want to feel better about ourselves, wouldn't it be preferable to focus our efforts on developing a different self-concept? Maybe that is the response. The other

self-image is one of self-compassion. In the next post, we'll look more closely at what it is and why it might be beneficial to raise our levels of self-compassion.
low self-esteem

Self-Respect do You Really Want To Know?

Gain greater self-assurance. You can conquer the world if you feel good about yourself. When you put it in writing, it sounds fantastic, and you just want the reader to conclude that you're right. Their lives are immediately changed, and I should feel secure and highly valued. It's another frequent issue I've observed with language directed toward teenagers.

This "sound advice" is offered to you, but it seems like the individuals delivering it have forgotten what it's like to be a teenager. Things are occurring so quickly right now, and they are coming at you from all sides. You make an effort to adjust, yet something else disturbs the status quo. Teens are the most susceptible to self-esteem problems due to the abundance of events that occur during these formative years of life. You are greatly affected by everything that occurs, and it just takes one thing to destroy your self-worth and confidence.

Much of it is focused on the planet and all of its events. But when you project a lack of concern, you also assume a large portion of that obligation. How come I would have to do that? Why should I give such things any attention at this time? It would be beneficial if you showed concern since a loss of confidence and self-worth will prevent you from accomplishing almost anything in life. Possessing these items allows you to expand your horizons and create a mental room that helps you overcome the challenges of adolescence. Thus, in this chapter, we will learn the true meanings of confidence and self-esteem as well as their distinctions. Next, we'll explore the reasons for your increased concern for these matters, and lastly, I'll demonstrate to you how to build an unwavering foundation of confidence and self-worth.

What Are Self-Confidence and Self-Esteem?

I confused self-worth with self-assurance for many years. That resulted from numerous conversations I had as a teenager about the need for me to have greater confidence in myself or to have a higher sense of self-worth. I just went with it because it sounded the same to me. However, I didn't understand that these meant different things until I was much older and did some research on the subject. Being highly confident does not always translate into having a strong sense of self-worth.

Self-Belief

Goal setting is a very effective technique that gives us both short- and long-term motivation. It helps us go toward the future we want and allows us to evaluate where we are in life right now. Consider it a road map that leads us to our intended location.

Setting goals and breaking them down into objectives helps us to know what has to be done. By doing this, we become active creators of the life we desire rather than passive recipients of life's events. Setting goals gives you the ability to take charge of your life and mould your destiny to fit your desires. Additionally, it develops virtuous practices that improve our development.

Setting goals can become a process of forming habits if done correctly. We can gradually incorporate new habits into our lifestyle by putting them into practice once a week or once a month. It changes from being a routine task to becoming a way of life. Setting goals also promotes in-depth analysis of our actions. It gives us a chance to reflect on the parts of ourselves or our bad behaviours that we would like to improve.

Establishing goals on a regular basis strengthens our resilience. We learn new skills and habits of thinking as we create objectives and strive to meet them. By doing things like joining a gym, seeing a mentor, or going to therapy, we provide ourselves access to a wealth of opportunities as well as priceless tools and support. Our path of self-improvement and expansion gives us the fortitude to take on difficulties head-on and go over barriers.

There are several goal-setting models and variants, from the three Cs to the three Rs of goal-setting. The process of sorting through these possibilities can be intimidating.

Recall that the objective is not to become paralyzed by the procedure. Whichever model you select, they're all aimed at assisting you in reaching your objectives. It takes time and reflection to develop and establish goals that are appropriate for your particular situation. During this period, getting the help of a life coach or therapist can be quite beneficial.

Setting Goals Is Essential

Goal setting is a very effective technique that gives us both short- and long-term motivation. It helps us go toward the future we want and allows us to evaluate where we are in life right now. Consider it a road map that leads us to our intended location.

Setting goals and breaking them down into objectives helps us to know what has to be done. By doing this, we become active creators of the life we desire rather than passive recipients of life's events. Setting goals gives you the ability to take charge of your life and mould your destiny to fit your desires.

Additionally, it develops virtuous practices that improve our development.

Setting goals can become a process of forming habits if done correctly. We can gradually incorporate new habits into our lifestyle by putting them into practice once a week or once a month. It changes from being a routine task to becoming a way of life. Setting goals also promotes in-depth analysis of our actions. It gives us a chance to reflect on the parts of ourselves or our bad behaviours that we would like to improve.

Establishing goals on a regular basis strengthens our resilience. We learn new skills and habits of thinking as we create objectives and strive to meet them. By doing things like joining a gym, seeing a mentor, or going to therapy, we provide ourselves access to a wealth of opportunities as well as priceless tools and support. Our path of self-improvement and expansion gives us the fortitude to take on difficulties head-on and go over barriers.

There are several goal-setting models and variants, from the three Cs to the three Rs of goal-setting. The process of sorting through these possibilities can be intimidating. Recall that the objective is not to become paralyzed by the procedure. Whichever model you select, they're all aimed at assisting you in reaching your objectives. It takes time and reflection to develop and establish goals that are appropriate for your particular situation. During this period, getting the help of a life coach or therapist can be quite beneficial.

THE THREE CARDS FOR SETTING GOALS.

The Three Cs of goal-setting—clarity, commitment, and consistency—act as cornerstones to direct and improve your path to goal achievement.

lucidity

Setting effective goals is based on having clarity. It entails developing an unwavering comprehension of your goals. You may set SMART goals—specific, measurable, realistic, relevant, and time-bound—when you have clarity in your goal-defining process. Setting precise goals gives you a clear aim to work toward and makes it simpler to gauge your performance and development. You can direct your efforts toward what matters most to you by making sure your goals are reasonable and pertinent to your aspirations and values. Time-bound objectives help you prioritize your tasks and give you a feeling of urgency.

Dedicatedness

To be truly committed means to decide to pursue your goals with all of your might. It involves developing a strong sense of resolution and drive to go above and beyond to achieve your goals. It entails continuing to be committed despite obstacles, disappointments, or diversions. You cultivate a robust, tenacious, and determined mindset when you are genuinely committed to your goals. This degree of dedication keeps you motivated and on course—even in the face of adversity.

Regularity

The secret to achieving your goals is consistency. It entails moving toward your goals with consistency and regularity. Establishing weekly or daily routines and behaviours that support your objectives is the key to consistency. Working for your objectives on a regular basis gives you momentum and allows you to advance gradually. Maintaining consistency helps you stay on task and prevents you from being sidetracked by distractions. You get a sense of dedication and follow-through that helps you go forward when you practice consistency. It makes it simpler to maintain your efforts throughout time by assisting you in creating a rhythm and flow in your movements. You build a strong foundation for success and make sure that every little step adds up to the bigger picture when you show up on a regular basis.

Have faith in yourself

Your life has a purpose, regardless of the struggles you have encountered or the things you were told as a child. You are capable of so much more than you could have ever dreamed of, and you deserve to adore yourself.

You discover an entirely new world when you have

confidence in yourself. Instead of restricting your options with a pessimistic

fixedmindset, you'll engage with your environment and other people with the

innate wonder and interest that stems from a development mindset. To help you

reach your full potential, here are some things you may do to boost your

self-confidence:

Dark tears: The despair that

seeps into the spirit.

A common emotion that is a component of the human

experience is sadness. When a person experiences unrequited love, despair can

seep into their spirit and send them into a deep emotional dark hole. In this

third chapter, we will examine how melancholy appears in the context of

unrequited love, as well as how it impacts the individual on various levels and

how to deal with it in order to promote emotional well-being and healing.

Sadness is a normal reaction.

Sadness is a normal and appropriate emotional reaction

when one is shown unrequited love. Tears and a general sense of melancholy are

manifestations of the great anguish that the disappointment and sense of loss

caused in the person. Sadness is an indication that someone is connected with

their deepest emotions and that their heart is digesting emotional anguish.

The burden of despair

A sense of hopelessness may surface in the midst of the

sadness that consumes the spirit, distorting the person's viewpoint. When one

is hopeless, it might be difficult to see a way out of their current situation

and toward emotional healing. It can be quite depressing and stressful to

believe that nothing will ever change and that your sorrow will never end.

Being alone while experiencing agony

Even in cases where helpful individuals surround the person, being sad can result in a profound sense of loneliness. An intense emotional detachment from the outer world can result from the sadness of unfulfilled love, making the person feel misinterpreted and alone in their suffering. This emotional loneliness may hamper emotional expressiveness and the healing process.

The requirement to let yourself experience

The person at this stage must give oneself permission to experience and communicate the melancholy that has invaded their soul. Repressing your sorrow and grief might slow down your recovery and make it more difficult to let go of unfulfilled love. Letting yourself feel depressed is a self-care practice and a means of letting go of the emotional baggage you are carrying around.

The function of emotional assistance

Support on an emotional level is crucial when someone is experiencing such intense sadness. Family, close friends, or professionals can offer a safe place to share grief and express sentiments. In times of extreme despair, having someone who confirms feelings and listens without passing judgment can be a comfort to the soul.

Managing discomfort in the shadows

Although it can be difficult, facing grief in the emotional dark is an essential step on the road to recovery. Seeking quiet, secure times for introspection may be beneficial for the person. You might be able to relate to his more profound feelings during these reflective times and have a better knowledge of him and the grieving process.

Overcoming the depressive barrier

Sadness has the potential to stand in the way of emotional development and healing. The person must search for strategies to get past this obstacle and let some light into their emotional shadows. One strategy to reduce sadness and create moments of emotional well-being is to engage in pleasurable activities, spend time in nature, meditate, or pursue artistic or creative endeavours.

The pursuit of purpose amid suffering

When a person experiences a deep melancholy, they may start to wonder why they are suffering. One can discover chances for spiritual and personal development in this quest for purpose. Deep lessons about life, love, and resiliency can be learned from sadness. Grieving people who find a purpose in their journey can feel more empowered and derive greater meaning from the experience.

The passage of time as a healing ally

The process of getting over the sadness of unfulfilled love takes time. When it comes to achieving emotional healing, time is a valuable ally. The person may get less depressed as the days and weeks pass, which will enable them to become more receptive to new experiences and feelings.

Embracing grief and soul healing

Letting go of emotional barriers.

Asking for emotional support.

Coping with suffering during periods of introspection.

Allowing oneself to feel and express melancholy.

A person can face sadness and heal their soul from it with enough time and care, creating new opportunities for emotional health and personal development.

Understand ADHD and How to Handle It.

The three main signs of ADHD are:

Inattention (inability to focus).

Impulsivity (rash, unexpected acts).

It is acknowledged that ADHD affects a person's capacity to function well in the workplace and school, build relationships with others, and go about their daily life. ADHD is thought to be a chronic, debilitating illness. If treatment is not received, children with ADHD may have low self-esteem and poor social functioning. Due to a general increase in criticism, adults with ADHD may experience excessive self-criticism, low self-esteem, and sensitivity to criticism.

2.5% of adults and 8.4% of children are thought to have ADHD. When school-age children exhibit symptoms of ADHD, such as disruptions in the classroom or difficulty with homework, the condition is frequently first diagnosed. Due to the fact that their symptoms manifest differently, boys are diagnosed with it more frequently than girls. Nevertheless, this does not imply that men are more prone to ADHD. Girls tend to be docile, while boys typically exhibit externalizing tendencies such as hyperactivity.

Recognition and Signals

Many kids may struggle to maintain composure, pay attention, wait their time, sit quietly, and control their impulsive conduct. Children that fit the diagnostic criteria for ADHD differ from typical children in that the former group has significantly worse symptoms of inattention, hyperactivity, impulsivity, and/or organization than would be predicted for their developmental stage or age. In addition to causing severe discomfort, these symptoms might cause issues at work, school, or in social situations. The symptoms that have been seen are not related to a lack of obedience or an inability to comprehend duties or directives.

Three primary forms of ADHD exist:

Generally, a presentation lacks focus

Most people behave in an impulsive and hyperactive manner.

A diagnosis is based on the existence of enduring symptoms that have developed over the previous six months. ADHD symptoms initially appear in young children, though they can be identified at any age. The symptoms must have been bothersome in a variety of circumstances and present at the time of diagnosis before the patient turns twelve. The symptoms could appear elsewhere in the house, for instance.

a little unfocused

The term "inattentive" describes problems with concentration, planning, and maintaining focus. If the patient frequently displays six of the following symptoms, or five if the patient is 17 years of age or older, they are diagnosed with this type of ADHD:

Makes thoughtless errors or neglects to closely inspect details when doing assignments at work or school.

Finds it difficult to concentrate when reading a lot or listening to lectures or conversations.

Does not finish assignments, duties, or tasks connected to their job (may start but quickly loses attention).

Having trouble organizing their work, managing their time, and meeting deadlines. They also struggle to maintain organization in their job and tasks.

Dislikes or despises intellectually hard chores such as writing reports and completing out paperwork.

Regularly loses items that are necessary for everyday chores, such as books, keys, wallets, cell phones, and spectacles.

Becomes distracted easily.

Overlooks routine chores like cleaning and errand running. Adults and older teens frequently forget to make phone calls, pay bills, and keep appointments.

Impulsive or exuberant personality

Hyperactivity is defined as excessive movement, which includes chattiness, fidgeting, having a lot of energy, and moving around while seated. Impulsive decisions or behaviours are made without planning. If the patient frequently displays six of the following symptoms, or five if the patient is 17 years of age or older, they are diagnosed with this type of ADHD:

Fidgets or squirms around in their chair, tapping their hands or feet.

Unwillingness to remain sitting (in a meeting or at a desk).

Runs around or exhibits inappropriate climbing actions.

Unable to play games or engage in quiet pastimes.

They were motorized, so they were always "on the go."

Talks too much.

Answers questions fast (e.g., by speaking during conversations or by concluding others' sentences).

Have difficulty waiting their turn, for example, in a line.

Interferes with or intrudes upon the privacy of others (for example, by beginning to use another person's property without authorization or by ending games, talks, or other activities). Adults or older teenagers may pick up tasks abandoned by others.

When a patient fulfils the diagnostic requirements for both the hyperactive/impulsive and inattentive types of the illness, a variation of ADHD is defined.

Mental health professionals or general practitioners frequently diagnose ADHD. A complete medical and mental health history; a family history; details on education, upbringing, and environment; a description of symptoms provided by the patient and caregivers; and the completion of scales and questionnaires by the patient, caregivers, and educators. In order to rule out any medical concerns, it could also involve a referral for a medical evaluation.

Tips For Developing Self-Esteem That Values You Both Internally And Outer

You can't achieve that if you keep comparing yourself to other people. When you compare yourself to other people, the first thing you'll notice is how much better they are than you, and if you keep doing this, you'll discover more and more reasons to be unhappy with your life. To love oneself is to embrace oneself without becoming egotistical or self-centred. Over time, it becomes a habit, making it impossible for you to evaluate yourself, your actions, or their consequences in an impartial manner. You completely lose faith in yourself and your capacity for success as a result of this behaviour because you stop believing in yourself. Assume for a moment that a company recruited you and that your colleagues in your division have already accrued vacations, cars, and apartments. What kinds of thoughts might come to mind when you see a situation like this? You may have more time, energy, or talent than anybody else in the organization because you are a recent graduate. Still, you unintentionally started viewing others as superior to you, which could seriously harm your self-esteem. You shouldn't expect others to accept you for who you are if you don't. Because of this, even with your advantages, you can begin to feel like a loser and that nothing in your life has been done. Stop comparing yourself to other people if you want to accomplish something for yourself. You can only compare yourself to the person you were in the past, and you can only compare yourself to the consequences of the past. Acknowledging your positive traits and realizing your value are essential components of inwardly and externally valuing oneself. This has the potential to significantly increase self-esteem because internal self-worth and a positive self-image are developed when one values oneself. This enables you to see yourself more realistically and fairly, emphasizing your advantages over your alleged disadvantages.

When you have an external self-worth, you look to other people for approval and confirmation of your actual value. This entails being in the company of those who value and encourage you, as well as participating in pursuits or goals that fulfil you and are consistent with your values. Your self-esteem is further boosted by treating yourself with internal and external values, as this reinforces the idea that you deserve of respect and favourable treatment from others.

Increasing your self-esteem can be achieved through valuing oneself on the inside as well as the outside. Here are a few ways it can be beneficial:

Internal approval: You can build a strong feeling of self-worth independent of other people's perceptions when you appreciate yourself on the inside. This entails acknowledging and celebrating your successes, skills, and talents. This internal validation enhances self-esteem and a good self-image.

Establishing Healthy Border

Establishing appropriate boundaries in relationships and interactions is facilitated by having an internal and external sense of value for oneself. It enables you to convey your requirements, stand up for yourself, and stop other people from taking advantage of you. This raises one's sense of respect and self-worth.

Establishing and upholding sound limits is essential to boosting one's self-esteem. Determine your priorities and values, and Think about your priorities and the things you will and won't put up with in your life. Establishing limits that are consistent with your identity and beliefs can be made easier by being aware of your priorities and values. Acquire the ability to refuse: Practice saying no without feeling bad about it or wanting to justify everything in great detail. Refusing requests or actions that conflict with your personal needs or values is acceptable. Setting limits and preserving your time and energy can be achieved by politely and guilt-free saying no. Share your boundaries with others. In order for people to know where you stand, be sure to convey your requirements, expectations, and boundaries to them politely and clearly. People may forget or unintentionally transgress your boundaries. Therefore, it's critical to communicate them often. When communicating, use assertiveness. To effectively communicate your boundaries, cultivate aggressive communication skills. When communicating your ideas, opinions, and boundaries, do so with confidence, clarity, and directness. Steer clear of passive or aggressive communication methods, as these might cause miscommunication and make it harder to set and enforce healthy boundaries. Decide on repercussions for crossing boundaries. It's critical to set repercussions for behaviour when someone consistently transgresses or disregards your limits. To make it clear that your boundaries are unassailable, communicate with others and enforce these repercussions. Establishing limits and preserving self-worth requires consistency.

Recall that assertiveness and practice are necessary for establishing and upholding boundaries. To safeguard your general well-being, wellbeing and sense of self-worth, practice self-compassion and consistently enforce your boundaries.

Accepting Who You Are: Self-acceptance and self-compassion are cultivated when you value who you are on the inside. You come to accept your vulnerabilities, defects, and flaws and realize that they don't define who you are. Having compassion and acceptance in oneself helps one feel more confident.

SATURNINE OFF ACHIEVEMENTS

When you place an external value on yourself, you recognize and commemorate your successes. You are proud of what you've accomplished and give yourself credit for your diligence and hard work. Acknowledging your accomplishments strengthens a good self-image, which raises self-esteem.

Enrolling in positivity: By surrounding yourself with supportive people and situations, you may prioritize your well-being when you value yourself both inwardly and externally. This entails avoiding harmful situations, looking for supportive connections, and partaking in joyful and fulfilling activities. Positive surroundings support the development of self-worth and confidence.

Building resilience is aided by valuing oneself on the inside as well as the outside. A strong sense of self-worth makes it easier for you to deal with obstacles, failures, and criticism. You have a higher probability of persevering through setbacks, keeping an optimistic mindset, and believing in yourself.

Because resilience enables people to overcome obstacles and setbacks, it is an essential part of developing self-esteem. Consider failures as instructive opportunities and modify your strategy accordingly. Recall that failing does not define you; it is an inevitable part of life. Build a network of allies. Be in the company of upbeat, encouraging people who will always have your back. Look for mentors, family members, or friends who will encourage you and believe in you when things are tough.

Develop your ability to solve problems. Divide difficulties into smaller, more manageable pieces to improve your problem-solving skills. Create a plan of action and look for innovative answers. Resilience increases with self-assurance in problem-solving skills.

Show appreciation, and You can increase your resilience and concentrate on the positive aspects of your life by adopting an attitude of appreciation. Consider and be grateful for the things in your life on a regular basis. This can assist you in changing your viewpoint when things are tough.

Use stress-reduction strategies; various methods, such as deep breathing exercises, meditation, or relaxing activities, can aid in stress management and improve resilience. You can achieve inner calm and maintain your sense of groundedness by using these approaches.

Being resilient helps you face life's obstacles head-on and boosts your self-esteem by enabling you to do so. Keep in mind that developing resilience is a continuous process that requires patience and experience.

Finally, valuing who you are on the inside as much as the outside might help you feel better about yourself. You may significantly improve your self-esteem and general well-being by acknowledging your values and skills, establishing sound boundaries, practising self-acceptance, celebrating accomplishments, surrounding yourself with positivity, and developing resilience.

Confidence: What Is It?

The capacity to face circumstances without your conscience telling you that you are inadequate is known as confidence. Your interactions with others radiate confidence. It's definitely not an ego issue. Unfortunately, many men misinterpret this, as women can identify a self-assured man at a glance and can see right away if you have issues that need to be resolved before you're ready for a relationship. It could be possible for them to tolerate your complexities out of desperation, but wouldn't it be good to date a lady fairly? Picture yourself feeling comfortable about being seen with the most poised and attractive woman in the room—a woman you date. She does not always express the feeling, yet it is possible. Whether or not she is with you, it should still make you feel good about yourself. I'll also be able to explain why. How can you expect to attract happy, confident women if you don't look like you do? As always, the first step starts with you and your degree of confidence.

Casanova exuded assurance. He exuded it. That implied that he was confident in his appearance and that ladies were aware of this. He didn't have to say sorry to be who he was. He didn't need to give them the impression that they were the reason he was here. In truth, if he had done so, he would have come off as insecure since four fundamental thinking attitudes determine one's level of confidence and which you should adopt in order to approach life:

1. I am to blame for everything that goes wrong in my life. I accept accountability for who I am.

2. Do you feel lacking in a woman's presence? You are, therefore, not prepared to be a Casanova. It all comes down to realizing your completeness, whether or not a woman is by your side.

3. What are your life's priorities? Self-care should always be the top concern. That does not imply self-centeredness. It entails not making the pursuit of women your life's ultimate goal. Casanova would tell you that his lack of need was what drew women to him if you were to meet

with him. A woman is always drawn to a man who doesn't seem to care whether they are around or not, as it makes them feel indispensable.

4. Are you aware of your attractiveness to women? You are not prepared to take on the challenge of becoming the next Casanova if you don't know. It is reasonable to believe that there is no possible reason why a lady might not find you appealing.

It would help if you had inner confidence, which is what we will teach you how to cultivate over the next few chapters. Fundamentally, you don't need to change who you are. You have to have more faith in who you are and alter the way you see yourself.

Essential Human Fears

There are eight different human fears, and it's amazing how much we all battle with the same things. We thus frequently put people on pedestals. We consider people like Rosalind Franklin of the Virgin Empire, Nelson Mandela, the Dalai Lama, Mother Teresa, OpprahWeinrey, and Barbara Walters. We consider these people to be courageous. We believe that some individuals are born with courage and are meant for greatness, while the majority of us must acknowledge and just respect them.

This is untrue. Every single one of you struggles with the same kind of fear.

Dealing with fear is part of being human. The secret is to identify your fears and take the necessary steps to overcome them.

You start working to transform them as you face them and flee from them. The common trait of successful people is that while feeling their concerns, they run away from them. They do not let their fears get in the way of their aspirations. It's really your grandmother coming to visit you, and it's interesting to see how, once you start confronting your anxieties, you start to let them go.

But when you do, other anxieties will surface. Your entire life is really just the inner labour of overcoming the anxieties that are unavoidably arising to meet you.

As you progress, your power increases, and you are able to conquer the next fear much more easily. This is because you can overcome every fear you encounter. You reach an entirely new degree of potential and beauty in your life.

Eight Fundamental Human Fears

1. The Aversion to Failure

No success is possible without failure. When you turn your back on failure, you keep yourself from reaching the success you really want. Those who succeed the most have actually failed the most.

You will need to accept the failure, and when it happens, you must pick yourself up, get back up, and move on. You have to consistently leave your comfort zone.

Try new things, dream big dreams, and seize fresh opportunities. FAILURE is essentially your market research. Take the risk if it's something you really want to do. Risk should be assessed based on the value of the goal rather than the fear it causes in you or the likelihood of your success.

2. The Success Fear

This is probably upsetting most people. You're thinking, "I want success, I want to be successful financially, I want to be successful with my family, and I want my business to be a huge success. I'm not afraid of success." I desire all of these things. I have no fear of it. Even though you might not be conscious of it, we frequently harbour subliminal fears about what success might entail for our lives. That it might need too much time or that it might give you too much responsibility.

Recognize bad intentions. We often give up on achieving our goals because we are afraid of the price we might have to pay.

3. The Illness of Rejection

This is the dread that keeps us from pursuing our desires. It's the fear that causes many people to agree on everything before expressing their opinions. Therefore, you frequently want to ask for something—whether it's in a friendship, a relationship, or a raise at work—but you just don't.

The annoying thing is that this mindset is frequently predicated on an assumption that isn't accurate. Should you manage to pull up the courage to request an upgrade to an in-line ticket, request that special table in a restaurant, or request a refund, you can very well receive the following response: "Yes, you deserve it; I didn't know you wanted it and we can definitely accommodate you."

Accept the risk, participate in the game, and use your courage to ask for what you desire. It is crucial to modify your dreams and politely inquire about what you desire. The Alchemist's author, Paula Kuelho, once stated, "What people think of us becomes more important than our destiny." Don't let that happen to you; chase your dreams and fulfil your destiny.

4. The Fear that One Is Not Good Enough

I believe we've all experienced this one. We assume that extremely successful people, such as top CEOs or athletes, couldn't possibly have any self-esteem issues. Subsequently, you discover that they actually do.

People frequently experience a fear of not being good enough, which is known as the "Imposter Syndrome." This is the impression that someone is going to discover that they are not very intelligent and have no idea what they are talking about.

5. The Absence of Scarcity

This can be a particularly damaging dread because of the belief that what you put out into the world is what the world will return to you. We leave life with who we are, not what we want.

An excellent illustration of this would be in a business where you are succeeding and the enterprise is growing extremely profitable. Even if you might be becoming well-known in your community, if you suffer from a generalized fear of public speaking, you will always be worried that your success will fade. You fear that your current financial situation won't last forever. Instead of continuing to provide excellent customer service, you're constantly concerned with the value of the dollar, and you cut corners to ensure that your profit margins remain high. In the process of doing this, you're actually lowering your chances of your business succeeding going forward by giving in to your subconscious fear of criticism.

Keep in mind that the majority of bulls have an abundance of mentality. They are extremely appreciative of what they have and believe that everything is sufficient for everybody.

6. The Fear of Alone Rather than trying to fill our lives from the inside out, we attempt to do it from the outside in. We are just hanging out with ourselves, getting in touch with who we really are, and not really comfortable. It is crucial

to keep in mind that nothing external can ever fill a hole inside. The greatest secret to happiness is to love, appreciate, and be at ease with who you are.

7. The anxiety of losing control

We all want to be in charge of everything in our lives, whether it's taking care of our kids, running our work office, or even choosing what our spouse wears!

Take charge! We hold on to this because it is associated with a fear of the unknown and a fear of losing control. We probably all know someone—we might even be one of them—who operates in what I would describe as a perfect, imperfect system. Everything needs to be absolutely flawless. It's enough to drive you crazy, but the parody needs to be alphabetized.

All of it stems from your fear of losing control. Don't waste precious moments of your life by meticulously documenting every detail of your body. You will be able to feel much more at ease in your life if you can consistently confront your fears and bring them into your conscious consciousness.

8. The concern of Being Different or Standing Out can be a very real concern since it frequently leads us to hide our true selves behind a social mask. We are not authentic; we do not live up to our true selves. Sometimes, we choose careers in accounting or medicine because our parents encouraged us to do

so. We marry a specific individual because we believe that person is what society expects us to be with if we want to appear successful. We don't truly love this person; it's only what we believe is rightfully expected of you.

This fear may lead us to believe the greatest lie that a human being is capable of believing: self-betrayal. Embrace who you are, follow your dreams, and live by your values and beliefs. This is what will make you happy. Live your life as you see fit. Make every effort to overcome your fear of what other people may think. I believe this to be Shakespeare's meaning when he wrote, "to thine own self be true."

Science Of Goodwill

Were you aware that kindness has a scientific basis? Kindness indeed has a hormonal effect. DacherKeltner, a UC Berkeley professor renowned as the "Kindness Scientist," researches the benefits of kindness. The assertion made by Darwin in 1871 that "Sympathy is our strongest instinct" is the basis of much of his study. He discovered that more compassionate cultures had a greater chance of success and more progeny. Keltner discovered that when people performed or watched acts of kindness, their levels of oxytocin and serotonin were elevated! These neurotransmitters release endorphins, aid in wound healing, and enhance well-being and social bonding. It's beneficial to your health to be kind! It's commonly known as the "love hormone" and occurs when two people cuddle. It lowers blood pressure, fosters a sense of community, boosts self-esteem, and encourages positive thinking, among other effects. Natural pain relievers called endorphins make you feel better about your body. Serotonin and dopamine activate your brain's reward region and provide you with a sensation of overall well-being and comfort known as the "helper's high."

Acts of compassion activate a network of neurons that already exists. In order to support improved health, the neurological system releases oxytocin when someone behaves with kindness and compassion. According to other research, compassionate people actually slow down the ageing process since they have twice as much DHEA as less compassionate people! Thus, we may also argue that kindness enhances our beauty! Significantly, it was shown that those who were compassionate had roughly 23% less cortisol in their bodies!

According to neuroscience research, experiencing pain triggers the same area of the brain as seeing someone else in misery. When we experience pain or witness someone else experiencing pain, our brains fire the same neurons. Moreover, it releases the same neurotransmitters that cause emotional or physical pain. Furthermore, it produces the same neurotransmitters when one is in pain or even imagines being in pain—this includes viewing a scary movie. These are important discoveries because they show that humans are designed to feel other people's sorrows and that our perceptions alone can affect how much pain we experience.

Recognizing Your Image

Your self-image serves as a reflection of who you think you are. In this chapter, we'll look at how your self-image impacts your self-esteem and how to raise it.

Self-image: What Is It?

The mental image you have of yourself is called your self-image. It's your opinion of your worth, abilities, personality, and looks. Your perception of oneself has a direct impact on your self-esteem and can be either positive or negative.

The Connection Between Self-Esteem and Self-Image

Your sense of self-worth and self-image are intertwined. You are more likely to have low self-esteem if you have a negative self-image. Conversely, a favourable view of oneself tends to boost self-esteem.

Elements that Influence Self-Image:

1. Past Experiences: Your self-perception may be impacted by trauma or unfavourable events. In order to enhance your perception of yourself, it's critical to address these events.

2. Comparison with Others: Having a bad self-image might result from continuously comparing oneself to other people. Recall that every individual is distinct.

3. Media and Society: These two groups can skew your perception of yourself by

constantly promoting exaggerated notions of success and beauty.

4. Comments from Others: Self-image can be negatively impacted by unfavourable remarks made by others. Recall that other people's perceptions of you don't always accurately represent your value.

Enhancing One's Self-Perception:

1. Develop Self-Compassion: Be nice and understanding to yourself, even when you make mistakes or encounter difficulties.

2. Positive Affirmations: To support a positive self-image, use uplifting affirmations. Say affirmations such as "I

am capable" and "I deserve respect and love."

3. Develop Your Skills: To feel more assured of your abilities, enhance your skills and talents.

4. Refrain from Overly Comparing: Quit evaluating yourself against other people. Instead, concentrate on developing yourself.

5. Surround Yourself with Support: Continue to have connections with those who affirm and encourage your identity.

Exercise in Practice: A Letter of Love to Yourself

Compose a love letter to yourself that emphasizes your positive traits, accomplishments, and best attributes.

Every time you need a boost to your self-esteem, read this letter.

Recall that you may mould and enhance your perception of yourself over time. Your self-esteem will rise in tandem with your efforts to enhance your self-perception.

In the upcoming chapter, we will talk about self-compassion and how crucial it is to developing unwavering self-esteem.

THE BASIS OF INNER AWARENESS

Have you ever wondered why some people carry themselves through life with poise and assurance while others have ongoing self-discrepancy? Something as basic and profound as self-awareness might hold the key to the solution.

Being self-aware involves more than just knowing what you enjoy and don't like. It also involves understanding your strengths and shortcomings, realizing your core values, and living a life that is consistent with who you really are. This alignment frequently has the effect of the final piece fitting into a jigsaw puzzle—everything clicks into place. However, how?

First, self-awareness assists us in determining our central beliefs. Values are the underlying beliefs that direct our behaviour; they are similar to the compass that helps us navigate life. We may make decisions that are in line with who we really are when we know what matters most to us. Without a map, it would be like embarking on a road trip without expecting to get lost or wind up somewhere unexpected. Understanding your beliefs is similar to having a road plan for your real life.

Second, it enables us to stand by our convictions in the face of criticism. When we know exactly who we are and what we stand for, we become unbreakable. We remain steadfast in our beliefs and don't waver in the face of every strong viewpoint. This confidence stems from a profound understanding of oneself, such that one's basic beliefs are unaffected by the judgments of others. It is not the result of arrogance.

Think about the transformation of a caterpillar into a butterfly. The caterpillar accepts change and grows because it knows that in order to realize its full potential, it must develop.

Self-awareness can act as a beacon, guiding us toward being true to ourselves and authentic in a culture that often wants us to follow the herd. It's a powerful and necessary instrument that enables us to live lives full of meaning, purpose, and joy—it's not just a trendy idea.

Compassion For Self-Reflection

As complementary twins, self-awareness and self-reflection both support and nurture one another. The strong desire to achieve self-knowledge, to understand the causes of our emotional reactions, and to realize why we respond a certain way to certain situations is a cornerstone of self-reflective practice. This is not just a straightforward path that we are travelling on. It is an interior journey in which our curiosity serves as the lighthouse that guides us through the maze-like complexity of our inner selves.

Though it may seem straightforward, this exercise helps us examine the "why" and "how" underlying our ideas and behaviours rather than simply accepting ourselves as we are (Schön, D. A., 1983). Recognizing the power of self-reflection means realizing how it may reveal hidden feelings, sort through confusing ideas, and illuminate the dark corners where ingrained prejudices and beliefs are kept. Deeper connections to our values, motives, and goals are made possible, and it gives us the chance to tune in to our innermost selves.

The three most important traits we require are open-mindedness, honesty, and courage. Accepting our flaws, embracing our biases, and facing our anxieties are all crucial stages towards personal development, despite the fact that they may be challenging and uncomfortable. The successes outweigh the difficulties by a wide margin. We develop self-awareness, clarity, and insight via reflective practice, all of which help us progress.

Taking Appropriate Risks

Rigorous versus Calculated Risks

"Think Rich, Grow Rich: Building a Mindset for Wealth Creation" has a chapter called "Embracing Smart Risks" that calls to the brave. Here, we take a trip that goes beyond simple prudence and into the territory of calculated daring. We examine the difficult balance between measured risks that reveal our way and reckless jumps that result in misery in a world where uncertainty frequently pulls at our desires. We find the insight to know the difference when we tread carefully on this fine line, cultivating a mindset that feeds on calculated risk-taking.

1. Making the Difference: Three Easy Steps

Step 1: Knowledgeable Analysis and Research

Start by conducting an in-depth investigation and risk analysis.

Recognize the elements that could affect the outcome as well as the variables and possible outcomes. A reckless risk frequently entails taking unwarranted jumps into the unknown, whereas a planned risk is based on information and a thorough grasp of the circumstances.

Step 2: Calculating the Ratio of Risk to Reward

Evaluate the project's risk-to-reward ratio. Compare the possible gains against the possible losses. A well-calculated risk presents a fair probability of significant returns relative to the possible drawbacks. Conversely, a careless risk carries an equal chance of devastating losses even though it may offer large benefits.

Step 3 of Chapter 2: Planning for Mitigation and Contingencies Create a solid mitigation strategy and backup plan to deal with unforeseen circumstances. A measured risk-taker foresees obstacles and has a clear strategy to overcome them. A backup plan and the ability to adjust to unforeseen events set responsible risk-taking apart from recklessness.

2. Developing a Three-Step Process for Sensible Risk-taking First Step: Developing Self-Awareness

Gain a thorough awareness of your vulnerabilities, risks, and strengths. Recognize your comfort zones and your willingness to push yourself. The basis for making choices that are in line with your strengths and goals is self-awareness.

Step 3: Establishing a Helpful Network

Be in the company of peers, mentors, and advisers who understand how to evaluate risks and take calculated risks. Getting involved with a network that offers advice and insights might help you improve your decision-making and take more assured risks.

The capacity to distinguish between prudent and irresponsible risk-taking and to cultivate an attitude that encourages wise risk-taking are essential skills in the quest for wealth growth. By following these steps, you'll be able to better manage uncertainty and build a foundation that will help you achieve more prosperity and success.

2.2 Getting Out of Your Comfort Zone in Chapter 2

First of all, Leaving Your Comfort Zone Behind A chapter titled "Stepping Out of Your Comfort Zone" appears in the grand book "Think Rich, Grow Rich: Building a Mindset for Wealth Creation," and it serves as a call to courage. In these pages, we explore the significant effects of stepping outside of your comfort zone and into the space where success blossoms and growth takes root.

As we go into the core of this chapter, we examine the transforming force that emerges when we summon the bravery to welcome discomfort in the pursuit of unmatched prosperity.

Comfort frequently turns into a cosy cocoon that we construct about ourselves in the midst of life's hustle and aspirations. However, the very best know that although the cocoon is warm, it can also inhibit growth. "Stepping Out of Your Comfort Zone" is a call to challenge the boundaries of what is familiar and cosy. It serves as a reminder that the most remarkable accomplishments come from the vast unknown rather than the safe shelter of regularity. We shed light on how to find the unrealized potential that lies outside the boundaries of familiarity as we work our way through the complexities of this chapter.

Here, we welcome the idea of discomfort and acknowledge it as the rich ground where creativity and resilience flourish. Stories of explorers who ventured into unknown lands allow us to see firsthand the amazing changes that occur when we exchange the commonplace for the extraordinary. "Stepping Out of Your Comfort Zone" promises a plethora of experiences that enhance our path, unexpected interactions, and fresh viewpoints. Come experience the joy of discomfort with us, as it holds the keys to unmatched development and success.

INSIGHTFUL ADVICE FOR CREATING SELF-ESTEEM

Have self-compassion and treat yourself with kindness.

Being nice to oneself is fundamental to having a high sense of self-worth; therefore, treat yourself with the same kindness that you would show to your loved ones or close friends. Be gentle to yourself instead of becoming upset or blaming yourself if you make a mistake or encounter a struggle since nobody is perfect, and everyone will fail at some point in their lives.

Determine your assets and celebrate them every day.

Always be aware of your advantages and value your skills, talents, and other good attributes. It strengthens your sense of self-worth and self-belief, which enables you to face obstacles and problems with greater assurance.

Make attainable goals and acknowledge your accomplishments.

Always aim for attainable objectives because every success provides you with a feeling of direction and purpose. If your goals are more ambitious, divide them up into more doable tasks and recognize each one as a victory. Celebrating your accomplishments helps you feel better about yourself and recognizes the work you've done to advance. It gives you self-belief that you can accomplish more ambitious objectives.

Be in the company of upbeat and encouraging people.

Being around people who support and encourage you may have a big impact on your self-esteem, so make an effort to surround yourself with positive individuals. Positive individuals in your life, such as coworkers, friends, neighbours, and relatives, can uplift you and give you a sense of community.

Affirmations can take the place of negative self-talk when it is challenged.

Speaking poorly about yourself will have a detrimental effect on your sense of worth. Therefore, if you find yourself thinking negatively, confront these beliefs and replace them with affirmations that uplift your self-esteem and remind you of your worth. For instance, replace negative ideas with affirmations if you find yourself thinking, "I always make mistakes." "I never make mistakes, and I am always correct."

Accept failure as a chance to learn.

Everyone experiences failures in life, but true warriors bounce back, take lessons from their mistakes, and keep battling until they succeed. Therefore, rather than being afraid of failing, use every setback as a chance to grow and better yourself. Consider what went wrong and how to do it right the next time you make a mistake.

Maintaining your physical well-being is crucial for having a strong sense of self-worth, so make sure you always exercise on a regular basis and eat a balanced, healthful diet. A healthy diet gives the brain the nourishment it needs, and being in good physical health boosts your confidence.

Sleep enough to help your body and mind recover.

A healthy sleep schedule enhances mental, physical, and emotional well-being. Your brain functions more clearly and enables you to efficiently manage stress when you get enough sleep. Inadequate sleep can have detrimental effects on one's physical and mental well-being, lowering self-esteem and impairing one's capacity for rational thought.

To record your thoughts and progress, keep a journal.

You can think about your own and make improvements by journaling about your ideas, feelings, and everyday behaviours. You are able to record your successes, failures, and personal development in writing. It can also assist you in recognizing your negative self-talk and swapping it out for empowering statements.

Live in the present and cultivate mindfulness.

Being totally present in the moment without passing judgment is the essence of mindfulness. By engaging in mindfulness practices, you learn to completely observe your thoughts and feelings without letting them control you. This will assist you in recognizing negative emotions and substituting them with uplifting affirmations. You also have no regrets about the past and no worries about the future since you are living in the now.

Reject praises with grace, but don't minimize them.

Rather than seeming haughty when someone compliments you, accept them with grace by grinning and saying "Thank you." This supports positive feedback, which raises your self-esteem, in addition to assisting you in realizing your value.

Keep your journey in mind and refrain from comparing yourself to others.

Instead of comparing yourself to other people, concentrate on your development and life's journey. Everybody has different aspirations. Therefore, you should measure your accomplishments against your aspirations rather than those of others. Your self-esteem might be damaged by comparing yourself to others.

How Much Do I Believe In Myself?

I enrolled in an art class during my first semester of college when I had an exceptionally embarrassing incident. I reasoned that it would be a great chance to broaden my views and learn different artistic mediums. I had no idea that the teacher would make us publicly grade each other's work.

We were required to take our completed projects outside into the hallway and hang them against the wall. Subsequently, we had to remove each piece individually, placing the two we deemed to be the best at the front and the worst at the back of the line.

Oh, the horror I felt at discovering my work of art at the end of the line! My self-esteem was destroyed by the notion that my classmates and fellow students believed my artwork was the poorest in the group. After my work and my self-worth were publicly exposed for all to see in the art department, I promptly stopped the class.

I wish I could say that experience was eventually behind me. Since then, though, I've lost confidence in my ability to sketch and draw. Even now, I still try to avoid showing anyone my artwork, and when I do, I usually say things like "I'm not very good" or "I'm not an artist." Seeing and hearing from people about my art again still makes my pulse race and my chest constrict. The worst thing is that I could have learned this ability, but I was deterred from attempting it because of the experience.

Hundreds of thousands of these isolated moments—both the good and the bad—form our sense of ourselves.

What Determines One's Self-Esteem?

Even while self-esteem originates from within, a complex interplay of social, psychological, and physical elements continuously shapes it. These are only a handful of them.

❖ The genetics that affect our hormones, pain levels, and other parts of our body

❖ Our age (hormones, biology, and the cultural expectations associated with it)

❖ Our sex and gender, particularly the cultural expectations ascribed by family and community.

Our upbringing, our health, our personality, and our life events, no matter how positive, negative, embarrassing, or terrible.

❖ Cultural norms ❖ Family and peer expectations ❖ Reactions to your hobbies, convictions, and abilities ❖ The degree to which your needs are satisfied ❖ Our dinner ideas

❖ Social seclusion, as the COVID-19 quarantine in 2020.

Certain events, like an unexpected victory or a quick loss, can send our self-esteem through transient highs and lows. Even though these fleeting highs and lows will soon return to the mean, very traumatic events have the power to alter our overall or domain-specific sense of self-worth.

A Major Factor in Both Our Global and Domain-Based Self-Esteem is Family and Upbringing.

Our sense of self-worth originates at home and has enduring consequences [7][8]. From the time we are defenceless babies in need of our parents' attention to survive to the norms and values we are exposed to as we grow up. Our family members then come to us as adults to share their views and opinions. They are always the yardstick by which we evaluate our values, accomplishments, and moral compass.

Positive self-identity development is facilitated in children in a healthy home setting when parents show their children unconditional love and acceptance. Additionally, people might feel more secure in their activities and the results they will get if they modify specific behaviours since they have consistent standards and criteria to measure their conduct.

Conversely, a dysfunctional family dynamic can adversely affect kids' self-esteem. Children who grow up in unloving or unaccepting homes or in families where love has conditions may find it difficult to feel good about themselves. Youngsters in these households could experience feelings of unlove and unappreciation, which could result in low self-worth.

These kids might be exposed to self-defeating messages like being told they are unworthy or incapable of reaching their objectives. The child may be affected by these harmful signals for the rest of their life. High levels of anxiety and doubt are also produced by an inconsistent environment where safety standards and regulations are often changing, making it harder to forecast future events.

Our sense of self-worth influences our ideas, attitudes, and actions. These are some key characteristics that indicate either a high or low level of self-esteem.

The Standard of Our Inner Dialogue

Everybody harbours an inner critic. The voice analyses situations and makes predictions.

Individuals who have low self-esteem have a very critical inner voice. Extremes and absolutes characterize the inner voice's speech. They cast blame, belittle you, cast doubt on your skills, and make issues appear intractable. Which of these seem familiar to you?

- "My math skills are too low." This test demonstrates my lack of competence.

- "It's unbelievable that I said that! Everyone now believes that I'm a jerk! I should just keep quiet and never speak during social events. I'm bad.

- "After a month, I'm still far from reaching my fitness objectives! For the rest of my life, I will be a lard."

- "Why was I not invited? Was there something I didn't do right? I must have made a mistake somewhere and failed to see it because I'm socially shy. I'm probably too dull to spend time with. Are they simply too polite to say anything because they detest me?

- "I made another mistake. I'm a screwup, and I will remain such forever.

- "This was a bad date. I'm awful.

"My supervisor is really a jerk." However, there is nothing I can do to stop them from making my life a living nightmare or firing me. All I can do is bite my tongue and hope that they quickly switch to using someone else as a punching bag.

An inner critic who is in good health tends to be more kind and impartial. In addition, they exhibit greater levels of self-compassion, a topic we will delve into further in the book. We are able to objectively and reasonably assess our strengths and weaknesses and precisely measure all the internal and external variables. The inner critic moves forward with a problem-solution strategy when we fail. With a more positive inner critic, the same statements above sound like this:

- "On the majority of these quiz questions, I misread my signs. I should perform better on the end-chapter test if I go over these indicators again.
- "I made a joke that was not appropriate. I'm sorry, but what I said cannot be taken back. I promise to be more careful about the jokes I post and their context in the future.

● "This week, I accomplished far more than I did last! I'll get there, even though I'm not quite where I want to be.

"I'm curious as to why I wasn't invited. Perhaps there was just a mistake, or there was a cap on how many people they could invite. To make sure there are no ill wills between us, I'll invite them for coffee because I truly appreciate our friendship.

● "I made a HUGE mistake this time, but it's not fatal." What actions are necessary for me to proceed?

● "My identity is not defined by one awful date. I'm capable of this.

● "While I can't stop a nasty boss, I can voice my concerns about their actions. I ought to go over the employee handbooks in case HR has to step in and mediate.

Where do most of your ideas come from? Does your self-criticism boost or lower your self-esteem?

Self-Belief

The capacity to trust and rely on oneself to handle various circumstances is known as self-confidence. Because of their strong ties, self-confidence and self-esteem always influence and support one another.

Low confidence and severe self-doubt are common among those with low self-esteem. When faced with a difficulty, individuals are more inclined to come up with reasons to remain in their comfort zones.

Individuals who possess a positive sense of self-worth tend to be more confident. They are more inclined to attempt something novel with no assurance of success or take a measured risk.

A Sense of Being in Charge

People who have low self-esteem could think they have no control over anything. Neither their work path nor their relationship can be altered. The reason they can't get better at talent is that "it's the way they are." A parent is unchangeable; therefore, setting limits and talking about painful subjects are pointless.

Conversely, those who struggle with low self-worth may be extremely afraid of losing control. To maintain control in circumstances like a relationship, group endeavour, or household money, they could act manipulatively.

What Self-Esteem Means

IT IS OFTEN RELATED TO THE PEOPLE AND SITUATIONS YOU ARE CONSTANTLY AROUND. Several factors can determine whether your self-esteem is high or low. These factors include:

Domestic Life

Your self-esteem is frequently greatly influenced by the bonds you have with your family. You spend a lot of time with these people from an early age, and you frequently begin to imitate their behaviours and attitudes. You are more likely to have stronger self-esteem and not judge yourself harshly based on others if your parents were emotionally mature and taught you that every individual is different and has special qualities. However, if your parents constantly made fun of your flaws or whined about how others were better than them, you could find it difficult to see your value, and your self-esteem would suffer.

School Life: Your time in school can shape a large portion of your self-esteem. The way your students respond to you will determine how you see yourself. After seeing what benchmarks are deemed exceptional or normal, you can assess whether you fall within this range. Many people who struggle with low self-esteem could think that they are not as popular, athletic, or attractive as their classmates and that they are on the outside looking in.

A lot of people depend on their sense of self-worth in their social circle. They can fear that they aren't as popular or well-liked if they notice that others seem to be more liked or if they get the impression that nobody wants to be near them. Pupils could be concerned about how their peers would see them, how they act, and how they dress. If they can't improve, they'll carry the same low self-esteem problems from when they were younger long after they graduate from school.

Community

Your self-esteem is frequently influenced by the relationships you have with people in society, especially those who have different religions, cultures, and racial backgrounds. You will be able to assess whether or not you live up to the various standards that are prevalent in these cultures. Those who are primarily exposed to one social group may find it challenging to maintain a high sense of self-worth if they happen to be a little bit different. They consider themselves strange or excluded because they haven't been exposed to a wide variety of people.

Media

The media has a big impact on your self-esteem in today's society. Many pictures exist of the "ideal" person, someone who is unreal but whom everyone feels they must aspire to be like. The media constantly dictates what we should wear, how we should behave, and every other aspect of our lives. Young people, in particular, may find it particularly simple to have low self-esteem when they don't meet these unrealistic and lofty expectations.

Younger children are highly susceptible to the influence of the media. Youngsters raised in an environment where television and the internet are prevalent are more accustomed to seeing these fictitious social effects. Compared to what they would find in their neighbourhood, they are exposed to more of this. They will find instances of people who are similar to them—people with ordinary bodies, issues, and attitudes—in their little social circles. However, the individuals to whom the younger generation aspires are not authentic. TV personalities and celebrities use money, plastic surgery, and made-up issues to attract viewers.

The problem is that a lot of youth, and even older adults, find it difficult to recognize this as being false. They believe that their favourite celebrity sets the perfect standard, and they feel compelled to live up to it. However, no average person can ever live up to the expectations of Photoshop, liposuction, and a whole beauty squad; instead, they will feel inadequate and unworthy when they fall short of this benchmark. Our self-esteem is greatly impacted by the way we are portrayed in television and other media. Thus, the best strategy to improve our self-esteem in this case is to minimize our exposure to these media and spend more time with actual people doing the activities we enjoy.

Additional elements

Additional elements that may impact how high or low your self-esteem is include:

• Feedback: all you learn from others in your immediate vicinity. You might hear things from individuals about you, how others treat you, what significant role models have to say about you, and even how others perceive you.

- Handling: how you decide to respond to events that happen to you.

- Success: Having more life triumphs increases the likelihood that you will have a high sense of self-worth.

- Popularity: How much other people like or dislike you might have an impact on your sense of self-worth.

- Image: How we think we appear to others, speak, or look can have a significant impact.

Most of the time, a combination of these variables will determine whether or not you have a high sense of self-worth. It could take some time to address a few issues before you feel truly secure in who you are.

COMMON FATHERLY MISTAKES IMPACTING A CHILD'S SELF-ESTEEM

"Praises and criticisms are not appropriate. Being sucked into one of them is a sign of weakness." John Wood

Every parent wants to see a rise in their kids' confidence and sense of self-worth.

A recent study did discover, nevertheless, that some things parents do for their children's benefit really have the opposite effect on their self-esteem. Specifically, our behaviour causes our kids to fear failing and distrust our honesty.

The five most frequent errors made by parents are typically the result of ignorance of the repercussions.

1. Making Use of Criticism and Approval

Making kids feel good about themselves is one of the keys to helping them develop self-esteem, and a lot of parents think that the best way to do this is to give their kids lots of praise and encouragement. While it is true that certain praise and encouraging remarks can help children grow, research indicates that some praise may actually be more detrimental than beneficial.

Actually, research indicates that kids are frightened to show off their "flaws" and act in ways that cast doubt on their "talent." Thus, praising kids and calling them "smart" or "good" can instil a fear of failing. Nonetheless, because it has been recommended by childcare specialists who have developed self-esteem over the previous 20 years, parents frequently utilize this kind of praise. By emphasizing children's "natural" talents over their capacity to learn new skills, using these evaluation phrases runs the risk of creating a specific identity in boxing. This is because if children believe they are "smart" or "good," they may feel pressured to perform constantly, which increases their fear of failing.

Because of this pressure to be "right," children are less likely to attempt new things or take chances, which prevents them from taking advantage of crucial opportunities to grow in confidence and self-awareness. They might become sceptical of their parents' genuineness and begin to disregard their gratitude.

Praise frequently has the opposite effect of what is intended since it makes kids concentrate on their flaws rather than their emotions.

For instance, our kids might respond this way when we tell them they are excellent readers. "How can I be a good reader?" I took twice as long as the other students in my class to finish the book." "My drawings from yesterday were much better, but I'm not sure why people are complimenting my paintings. They had to be telling lies."

Additionally, it causes mistrust and immediate denial. It might, in certain situations, feel like an operation. "I did nothing that they should be praising me for. They must want something from me, which is why they are saying that."

Even when the best intentions are behind it, evaluative praise just causes discomfort and undue pressure on kids to conform to their idealized view of their own "talent" and aptitude. As a matter of fact, a lot of parents believe that the more they try to give their kids praise as they become older, the quicker they get rejected.

That does not imply that we ought to stop praising our kids. Actually, the reverse is true. Developing a "growth mindset" requires using praise more effectively, as we will see in the upcoming chapter.

2. A focus on outcomes

When parents praise their children with phrases like "I'm proud that I've passed 100 per cent of the school examinations," they tend to focus on the outcomes and let their failures get in the way of their efforts. As we'll see in the upcoming chapter, their efforts and any mistakes they may make when something isn't "right" are typically more valuable learning experiences than the actual outcomes.

Furthermore, students who receive good grades are expected to be flawless all the time; if they are not, they will fail. Children who experience constant pressure to perform may develop a fear of failing in the long run.

It can also lead to youngsters believing that they won't receive praise from their parents unless they achieve the desired outcomes (winning football games, getting excellent exam scores, etc.). Furthermore, a lot of kids interpret this seeming lack of praise as criticism.

3. For Youngsters Who Compare and Criticize Others

Being continuously reprimanded for one's eating habits and receiving constructive feedback is the most disheartening thing there is. This enables them to be selected in a way that suggests they are embarrassed by their uniqueness and actions.

But it's really simple to fall into the error detection or disability detection mode as a parent, particularly if your child is sluggish and doesn't feel like they're putting in enough effort or engagement in activities. This is particularly valid for grades and tests. Finding errors in exams is fascinating, especially for younger students.

Rather than concentrating on what your child has done poorly, you will feel more confident and capable of making improvements. Don't allow feedback to undermine your self-confidence if you need it. See Chapter 3 for further details on how to accomplish this. Additionally, you ought to refrain from evaluating yourself against your siblings and schoolmates. Additionally, this deters motivation and may convey to kids the idea that they are flawed from birth and cannot improve much.

Discovering Your Personal Story

Examining and challenging our inner narrative—the ideas, opinions, and perceptions we have of ourselves—is essential to fostering self-esteem. We will go over detailed methods in this chapter to assist you in discovering your inner story and creating a more empowered and positive self-image.

First Step: Introspection

Make time for introspection and self-reflection. Locate a peaceful, cosy area where you may reflect deeply on your identity and ideals.

Step 2: Recognize Your Negative Inner Voice

Take note of your inner monologue and pinpoint any self-defeating thoughts. Take note of the negative and self-defeating ideas that start to cross your head. To bring them into your conscious awareness, put them in writing.

Step 3: Disprove Negative Thoughts

After recognizing your negative self-talk, confront those thoughts. Do these beliefs have a basis in reality? Are they just conjectures, or does evidence support them? Change your negative beliefs with ones that are kinder and more logical.

Step 4: Make Self-Compassion a Practice

Practice self-compassion by being nice and understanding to yourself. Recognize that everyone errs and encounters difficulties.

Treat yourself to words of support and encouragement, just as you would a close friend.

Step 5: Adopt Constructive Confirmations

Create uplifting statements to combat negative self-talk. Make declarations that showcase your abilities, qualities, and deservingness. To retrain your subconscious mind and reinforce positive self-perception, repeat these affirmations every day.

Step 6: Edit Your Narrative

Think back on the stories you have created around the events in your life. Determine which self-limiting or negative stories you have told yourself. Change those stories to emphasize development, resiliency, and individual agency.

Step 7: Seek Support. Speak with dependable family members, friends, or experts who can offer guidance and support. Talk to them about your experience of discovering your inner story and ask for help in refuting and confronting unfavourable assumptions.

Step 8: Be in the company of uplifting people

Consider the individuals and media outlets you spend time with. Assemble a supportive network of people who encourage and uplift you. Take part in positive and self-empowering activities, read books, or tune in to podcasts.

Step 9: Show Appreciation

Develop an attitude of thankfulness by taking time each day to consider the positive aspects of your life and yourself. Every day, list three things for which you are thankful, emphasizing your accomplishments and abilities.

Step 10: Writing Diary and Expressing Oneself

Write in your journal on a regular basis to examine and communicate your feelings.

Step 11: Adopt a Growth Mentality

Adopt a growth attitude and have faith in your capacity to develop, learn, and get better. Accept obstacles as chances for personal development and see setbacks as stepping stones to achievement. Place more emphasis on the learning process than just the final product.

You can start to discover and change your inner story by doing these steps. Recall that developing self-esteem is a continuous process that calls for perseverance, self-compassion, and steady work. If you remain dedicated to cultivating an affirming and empowering view of yourself, you will experience profound shifts in your sense of self-worth and general well-being.

The significance of fostering self-assurance

Adolescence is marked by a multitude of rapid changes that occur nearly simultaneously. Teens' social lives, academic achievement, environments, cognitive capacities, health, and physiological changes are all observed to have changed. Teens may find all of this to be extremely stressful, and it can be made worse if they don't have a confidant with whom they feel comfortable discussing their worries.

One of my lecturers once mentioned that when most guys start having wet dreams and most girls start their menstrual period, one of the most noticeable things they have in common is a peculiar sense of disconnection from the group of childhood buddies they used to hang out with. Suddenly, especially if those pals are not going through similar biological changes, they begin to feel as though they don't belong with the childhood buddies they used to play happily with. The drive to discover who you are becomes overwhelming. When loneliness sets in, the pressure to fit in and feel good about yourself increases.

It goes without saying that most teenagers find it challenging to adapt to and welcome the tornado of changes encircling their developing minds and bodies on a daily basis, even while some embrace this stage with excitement and joy. I've seen how the way a lot of teenagers view themselves causes their self-esteem to rapidly decline. Many girls would primarily judge their value and beauty based on the appearance of their faces and bodies. However, a lot of boys would base their self-confidence on their macho appearance, their powerful and deep voice, their athletic prowess, and the kind of girls they seemed to draw. Teenage years bring about a heightened desire for validation, which leads to the development of various coping techniques, some of which are problematic.

Teenagers rapidly discover how erratic they become when puberty sets in. Your hormones govern your reasoning and have a significant impact on your decision-making process, not reason. You start to doubt yourself after making a string of poor choices because of what your hormones are telling you. It is challenging to find validation in yourself when you are simultaneously having identity issues. You begin to turn to the outside world for validation that you are essential, competent, worthwhile, attractive, and good enough. The individuals you depend on the most to provide you with this validation and affirmation are your primary caregivers. Unfortunately, some parents or other caregivers aren't always aware of what their adolescent child needs, so occasionally, they may get used to responding in a way that leaves you feeling invisible and invalidated.

Imagine experiencing your first breakout and hiding away in your room for hours on end, terrified that your family and other strangers will discover you. Reassurance, love, and empathy—more than anything else—are what you need to hear when you eventually get up the guts to walk out and realize that, despite your breakouts, you are still beautiful. Instead, if you are greeted with cruel, insensitive jokes and remarks about your appearance, it can seriously damage your self-esteem and self-belief. This is the phase where the natural confidence and carefree attitude that all individuals possess begin to diminish dramatically.

When did you ask someone out and receive your first rejection? Or perhaps you tried to flirt, but they didn't seem to be interested in you back when you had a major crush on them? What emotions did you experience? It can be extremely unpleasant and demoralizing, and it might instil self-limiting beliefs in you that you had never before had. You can begin to see that rejection as proof that you are not attractive or attractive enough, insufficiently smart or talented, or that you don't measure up. The more bad things that happen to you while you navigate the issues of adolescence, the more these thoughts may come to mind. Your mind starts to integrate those recently formed unfavourable thoughts into your identity. Your self-esteem is severely damaged the more you adhere to those views and act in accordance with them, which causes numerous issues in all facets of your life.

Developing your self-confidence on purpose is really important, and it would be ideal if you made the time and effort to educate and rehabilitate yourself. The restrictive programming that governs your life as a fragmented self-esteem adolescent will continue to replicate the negative consequences that you no longer wish to encounter. You can take unwavering actions to draw the kind of life you desire—one filled with strong, fulfilling relationships and contagious self-assurance. This book will assist you in beginning the ascent to your new life and ultimately provide you with the opportunity to feel confident in your skin!

We will now go into great detail about the importance of cultivating and mastering self-confidence. It's crucial to determine how investing in a goal will impact your life before devoting time and effort to it. Now, let's get started!

Part 5 of "How to Become an Empowered Introvert" will explore the journey of discovering your energy and applying your reflective strengths to attain professional success. Your unique, considerate qualities can be quite helpful in determining a fulfilling career path that aligns with your preferences, principles, and objectives.

Examining Your Passions and Capabilities: You have to accept your interests and abilities before you can find your passion. Consider physical activities that provide you happiness and fulfilment. Your considerate disposition can improve your abilities in writing, creating handicrafts, analyzing data, and assisting others. Recognize and follow your passions as a path to a real and satisfying job.

Using Introverted Strengths to Your Advantage at Work Numerous strengths of introverts are highly advantageous in the business. Your ability to focus for extended amounts of time, think deeply, and listen attentively enables you to be successful in tasks that call for critical thinking, investigation, and attention to detail.

Examining Careers Suitable for Considerate People

Contemplative personalities are especially valued in a variety of occupations. Think about disciplines like writing, graphic design, computer programming, counselling, and scientific research. These careers often provide incredible opportunities for solo work, enabling you to thrive and take on significant responsibilities by leveraging your unique withdrawn traits.

Putting Up a Legitimate Front

Although organizing is an essential component of career success, lonely people may find it difficult. When it comes to systems administration, always keep higher standards in mind and concentrate on forming genuine relationships with like-minded individuals. Look for systems administration events that align with your interests and principles so that you may participate in meaningful dialogues.

Examining the possibility of new employee screenings

Screenings for new hires can be nerve-wracking, especially for considerate individuals. Prepare yourself fully by learning about the company and the role, and practice answering common questions. Highlight your strengths and unique qualities, emphasizing how these contribute to your value as an association resource. Remember that meetings could be doors that open for businesses to realize the value you bring, so confidently showcase your independent qualities.

Striking a balance between cooperation and introversion: Even though introverts prefer to work alone, professional teamwork is usually necessary. Determine ways to modify your need for alone time in a feasible, coordinated manner. Participate in collaborative initiatives that have good communication and support snapshots of focused work as needed to get re-energized. Find a balance that allows you to contribute meaningfully while honouring your introverted tendencies.

Accepting Persistent Education

Adopt a mindset of constant learning and skilful event handling. For introverts, self-improvement is a natural aspect of the growing process because they like delving deeply into subjects that pique their interest.

Increasing Self-Belief in Your Knowledge Even though it may be difficult for an introvert to stand up and share information, developing confidence in one's knowledge is crucial for career success. Engage in dialogue, share insightful information, and share your opinions with your peers.

Recognize the value of your knowledge and expertise, and have faith that your reflective nature elevates your obligations.

By embracing your introverted skills and finding your passion, you may create a successful and rewarding job that is in line with your genuine self. Remember that your reflection is a powerful tool that, properly used, may lead to professional success, self-improvement, and a sense of purpose in the career path you have chosen.

Carl Gustav Jung, a Swiss psychiatrist known as the "father of analytical psychology" and Jungian analysis, coined the term "self-realization." He was also a leading proponent of several groundbreaking ideas, such as "individuation" and "extroversion vs. introversion." Analytical psychology examines how one's behaviours, ideas, and actions reveal one's actual potential and focuses on bringing the subconscious mind into cognitive awareness. (Source: Merriam-Webster)

Realizing one's potential is not about coming to a definitive conclusion about it; rather, it is about realizing that one can never arrive at a definitive conclusion. In actuality, we are unaware of our immense potential. People constantly push the boundaries of their potential. As a species, we are singular in that we keep finding fault with our bounds. History has demonstrated that our mental restrictions actually dictate our potential for achievement, much more so than the physical limitations imposed by our bodies.

In 1954, Roger Bannister became the first person to run the "4-minute mile." Prior to his accomplishment, specialists believed that it was physically impossible for a person to run a mile in under four minutes and that the human body could never sustain such absurd circumstances. Because of this, everyone believed it to be a really foolish concept that may be fatal, so why even try?

Two more Vancouver runners completed the 4-minute mile just two months after Bannister's feat. More than 1400 athletes have completed a mile in under 4 minutes since then. Male middle-distance runners now use it as a benchmark.

When Roger Banister accomplished what everyone said was impossible, nothing about the human body's physical capabilities altered. Our perception of whether it was physically possible to complete a mile in less than four minutes was altered. By challenging then-accepted "facts" and opening a new path, Bannister disproved this notion for all of humanity and broke down mental barriers.

Limiting beliefs, or thinking that we are capable of less than we actually are, is a survival strategy that keeps us safe from potentially harmful situations. In an effort to keep us alive and safe, our brain warns us to avoid situations with high risks and great rewards. However, the preservation of our physical form takes precedence in our brain, leading to ideas that are frequently overly pessimistic about the true potential of our true selves.

Psychoanalyst Donald Winnicott developed the idea of the "authentic self" in the 1960s. The initial condition of being—the state of just existing, of being alive, of breathing air and pumping blood—is the real self. The true self is spontaneous, unplanned, and unadulterated. Consider this: infants don't conceal or alter their experiences in any manner. They are easily observable to others, and their feelings flow through them.

But as we begin to realize that, as biological beings, we actually can't just do whatever we feel like doing in this overly complex system of demands we call human society, we start to build the false self as a protection mechanism. Thus, we pretend to be polite in order to feel welcomed and suppress our anger. Kindness is a self-serving adaptive trait, according to Sigmund Freud's contentious claims (Kriegman).

Three years later, Anna Freud, his daughter, revealed the "egoistic gratification" of generosity in a much-regarded analysis (Richmond). They both believed that we hide our true selves from other people because we are members of a highly social species that depend on one another to survive and that the reason we are able to put on an act and conceal our basic nature is what makes us so advanced—it lets us take advantage of the resources in our surroundings.

The drawback, though, is that the need to fit in with society instils in us a "fear of exploitation" that intensifies with time since the further we deviate from who we really are, the more complex the mask we must wear.

The process of gradually removing the layers of fabrication is known as self-realization.

We are no longer carried away by the delusions of the false self when we learn to accept ourselves for who we are—light and dark—even though occasionally we will still need to pretend to be happy and say "thank you" without truly feeling grateful, or control our instincts to fit in with social acceptance. Living life according to one's principles and concept of success rather than the expectations of others is made possible by self-realization. It enables us to set objectives and cultivate values that uphold and advance our standards alone.

DefinitionOf Self-Esteem

One of the most crucial things in our lives is our sense of self-worth. It influences our feelings, thoughts, and actions. It's your perception of who you are. It's your level of self-worth and confidence in your skills. Everybody has varying degrees of self-esteem, and these can fluctuate based on circumstances and throughout a lifetime.

In general, those who have high self-esteem are confident in their skills and abilities. They are aggressive, upbeat, and self-assured. They are more inclined to attempt new things, take chances, and work toward their objectives. They also tend to bounce back from setbacks and show resilience in the face of difficulty.

Individuals who have poor self-esteem may have self-doubt, feel worthless, or belittled by others. They could be reticent, timid, or unsure. They might refrain from aiming high and taking chances. They also tend to give up more quickly and find it more difficult to bounce back from failures.

Self-Estimation Types

Learning the various forms of self-evaluation is the first step toward achieving high self-esteem. Global, domain-specific, and task-specific self-evaluations are the three main categories.

- A widespread feeling of value is known as global self-esteem. It is your assessment of who you are as a person overall. It provides us a sense of community and boosts our self-esteem.

- How you view yourself in particular contexts or domains of your life is known as domain-specific self-esteem. It encourages us to strengthen any areas in which we might be deficient.

- Task-specific self-esteem is the belief in your capacity to carry out a particular task or reach a particular objective. Since it is a trait that demonstrates how you accomplish goals, it is especially pertinent to the development of high self-esteem. Setting and completing goals helps you develop a strong sense of self-worth and confidence.

The majority of people lie in the middle of these two extremes. If we had to choose between the two, we would either get comfortable or feel helpless and overwhelmed.

Important Elements of Self-Esteem

Self-esteem is made up of several distinct yet important parts. These consist of • Self-efficacy, • Self-concept, • Emotional responses to oneself, and • Conduct toward others.

Every one of these elements works in concert with the others to form an individual's overall sense of worth.

• Your mental picture of oneself is known as your self-concept. It encompasses your outward look, character attributes, aptitudes, and place in society. Your self-concept influences your perception of yourself and your interactions with others.

• The conviction that you can fulfil your potential and accomplish your goals is known as self-efficacy. It entails having confidence in your skills and abilities, even in the face of difficulty.

•The feelings you have for yourself are your emotional reactions to yourself. These could be favourable or unfavourable. Emotional responses that are positive result in high self-esteem, while those that are negative result in low self-esteem.

• Your actions toward other people reflect your behaviour toward them. You will behave confidently and with respect toward other people if you have a strong sense of self-worth. Conversely, though, you might come across as aggressive or bashful around others.

THE NEGATIVE PERCEPTIONS LINKED TO EMOTIONS

The way you have been taught about emotions is intrinsically tied to how you feel them. There were a lot of experiences as an infant that you were unable to explain. You used to cry when hunger struck for the first time. You used to cry when you were too hot or too cold. You knew no other way to react than that.

Your parents, or any other adults in the room, would next try to calm you down as they try to figure out what set off your emotional reaction in response to your frightened cries. They fed you if you wept because you were hungry. They covered you with extra clothing if you were cold.

These were the early encounters that shaped your understanding of emotions and the many situations you encountered. Your brain learns that it's acceptable to experience hunger when you cry out for food, which is why you feel so much better after consuming it.

You continued to learn about the various feelings and emotions you had as a child, as well as the appropriate actions to take in response to those feelings. Having the proper support network around you made the process of learning much easier during this journey. The people that were there to guide you were parents, adults, and other caretakers, and they did their best. However, they were unable to read your mind, so they weren't always able to determine the precise feeling you were experiencing or the best course of action. You were, therefore, forced to search elsewhere to close these gaps in your understanding of emotions.

Where can we go for these other sources of information? The media is one source of information, but it's not the greatest one to depend on. The issue with gaining knowledge via the media is the exaggerated expectations and depictions of pictures. Examine the closest available source directly from your digital gadget. Social media platforms. It's impossible to ignore or completely avoid seeing photos, videos, and other stuff on your newsfeed of individuals who appear to have ideal lives. On these platforms, only happiness, excitement, or humour are permissible feelings. Any other feeling beyond happiness is frowned upon and shown negatively. It's common to see angry people as dangerous or even violent, yet depression and anxiety are seen as such taboo subjects that nobody wants to talk about them.

The ability to recognize, manage, and control our emotions begins to deteriorate as we get older. We are being taught to repress our feelings or not talk about them at all rather than acquiring healthy coping mechanisms for dealing with them. All too frequently, statements like "you'll be fine, don't think about it," "get over it," "put on a brave face," "don't show emotion, you'll be perceived as weak," and "you're making too big of this" have the same effect. The failure to control your emotions, much less master them. We've been brainwashed to believe that showing emotion is a sign of weakness. That it is improper to display emotion in public and that some individuals find it awkward to discuss emotions in public. Given such a mentality, is it any surprise that we repress our feelings to the greatest extent possible? Even when we know that's the wrong course of action, we nonetheless follow it as it's the simplest.

Aside from one issue. When you were younger, did you ever try to push a beach ball under the sea and use all of your strength to keep it there? Just to have it spring back up as soon as you released the ball from the pressure? You're performing the same thing with your emotions in place of a beach ball right now. Your emotions will bounce back quickly when you release the pressure, and the results aren't always pleasant.

Acknowledging the Importance of Self-Awareness

The cornerstone of personal development and overcoming codependency is self-awareness. It involves making a connection between one's ideas, feelings, behaviour, and underlying motives. Self-awareness becomes crucial in the context of codependency recovery because it enables people to identify the patterns that underpin codependent behaviours and, in turn, gives them the power to take control of their lives.

In addition to outlining the importance of self-awareness in the codependency recovery process, this section provides helpful strategies for fostering self-awareness, like journaling for self-examination and practising mindfulness.

Reflective Practice and Mindfulness

The therapeutic benefits of mindfulness, which have their roots in ancient traditions such as Buddhism, are becoming more widely acknowledged in contemporary psychology. It entails learning to live completely in the present moment, judgment-free. Within the framework of codependency treatment, mindfulness is a powerful tool for self-awareness. This is how it can be useful:

1. Observing Inner Processes: Mindfulness trains people to pay close attention to their thoughts and feelings as they arise. The identification of the underlying patterns that underlie codependent actions is made easier by this increased awareness.

2. Recognizing Triggers: Mindfulness helps recognize the situations or people that set off codependent emotions. Mindfulness assists in identifying these triggers, which may include the urge to

solve other people's issues, the fear of abandonment, or the need for approval.

3. Overcoming Automatic Reactions: Codependent behaviours frequently result from automatic reactions to particular circumstances. Being mindful gives you the room and knowledge to choose more positive answers in place of these automatic ones.

4. Understanding Emotions: Codependency is greatly influenced by emotions. By enabling people to go deeply into their emotions, mindfulness promotes a better understanding of the causes of these experiences.

5. Promoting Self-Compassion: Self-compassion is a critical component of codependency recovery and is fostered by

mindfulness. It makes it easier to develop a nonjudgmentalmindset toward oneself, which reduces self-criticism and self-condemnation.

www.ingramcontent.com/pod-product-compliance
Lightning Source LLC
Chambersburg PA
CBHW052134110526
44591CB00012B/1714